What God Has Joined . . .

Elisabeth Elliot

GATEWAY TO JOY

BOX 82500
LINCOLN, NE 68501

What God Has Joined . . . *Copyright © 1983 by
Elisabeth Elliot. First appeared in* Christian Herald
*magazine. Used by permission of the author. Published by
Good News Publishers, Westchester, Illinois 60153.*

Cover photo: Bob Mead

First printing, 1983.

ISBN 0-89107-276-4.

Publisher's Foreword

Issues of marriage and divorce are frequently debated today—with divorce too often viewed as an easy answer to marital distress. Unfortunately, these complex issues can be reduced neither to convenient exits from a difficult situation nor to simple formulas of successful home life. But there are divine guidelines specifically designed to encourage and renew, guidelines often minimized or overlooked.

Because Elisabeth Elliot in these pages (originally published as articles in *Christian Herald*) addresses the subject with a rare combination of unyielding commitment to biblical standards and personal concern, we enthusiastically include this publication in our book line.

It is our belief that the honesty and yet understanding of this booklet will bring strength to many.

What God
Has Joined . . .

To a Man Who Chose Divorce

May 1982

Dear Dick:

It was like a kick in the stomach to hear that you decided to get rid of Sally and the babies. We had heard some months ago that there was trouble. We did not know the nature or the seriousness of it, but we prayed. You opted for divorce and now it's all over. Or is it? You have your "freedom," such as it is, you live in the bachelor officers' quarters, and you can do what you like, without sacrifice or responsibility, while Sally is looking for a job and her parents have stepped in to help with the job you once promised to do—taking care of your wife and your babies.

I wrote to you, asking you to call, but no call came. I can understand why you did not want to talk to me or anyone else who might try to talk you out of what you had made up your mind to do. Your explanation for the decision, I am told, was that you did not want to be a husband, you did not want to be a father. As simple as that. But very poor timing, if I may say so.

"Wait a minute," you say, "you don't know the whole story." That's true. There is much on each side that I know nothing about. But I know this: you took a vow to cleave to Sally in sickness or in health, for richer, for poorer, for better *or for worse,* as long as you both should live. What did you think you meant by those words? A real man (that is, a true man) is always a man of his word.

You are a child of your generation. I can hear your answer: "But I've changed. Sally's changed. She's not the woman I married. I'm no longer the same man who mouthed those words (and they were only words, a tradition, a ceremony we went through to satisfy society). Things have happened to alter everything. Will you get off my back?"

You have grown up in a time when people are declaring their independence of what they choose to call "other people's morality." "What right do they have to tell me what to do? I have to do what's right for *me*," they whine, as though selfishness may be destructive for one man and constructive for another, as though putting the happiness of another before your own really need not be a part of the marriage contract in the 1980s.

You have your freedom, I said a moment ago, but it is only a manner of speaking. There is no freedom anywhere in the universe apart from the freedom we were created for in the very beginning: to glorify God. I'm not telling you anything you have not grown up knowing. You know also that the choices in life resolve themselves ultimately to this one: God or self. You are searching for some place in God's world where you need not face so stark a choice. You will never find it.

You have supposed that you can elect to stop being a husband and father. It is like saying, "Stop the world, I want to get off," because the truth is that you and Sally became one flesh. Divorce papers do not undo that. You begot two sons. Abandoning them cannot nullify your fatherhood. Your children will always be yours, and they will always know that you discarded them. I have no idea what the legal arrangements are, whether you have "visiting rights" or whatever, but no matter.

Those are nothing more than legal arrangements. The cold fact stands that you rejected the gift of fatherhood along with the gift of being husband and head and priest in the home you chose under God to establish.

"Sally can marry somebody else," you are quoted to have said. Perhaps she will. Your children will then have a stepfather who may love them as you ought to have loved them, and accept responsibility for their care which you have shrugged off. No protests that you love them, that you do indeed want to see them from time to time and pay their bills, can ever change the fact that you quit. Things were tough, so you bugged out.

You are in the military service now, Dick. Things might get tough there, too, but I would imagine you were sworn in. You pledged your word to serve, to obey the rules, to be loyal. Have we, the citizens of the United States, any reason to expect you to keep your word if you find, after a while, that you've changed, circumstances have changed, things were not exactly what you bargained for? Will you confront the difficulties by breaking the promises you swore to keep? Is your word to your country worth any more than your word to God, or to the witnesses before whom you plighted your troth to Sally?

You are holding imaginary dialogues with

those who condemn your action (people like me), proving that you had to do it, you couldn't take it any longer, it will turn out all right in the end, it will be much better for Sally and the boys. I hope you *are* holding such dialogues, because it would show that you needed to justify your action. Action that is clearly right needs no justification.

I dare to hope, too, that in some predawn hour of sleeplessness in your solitary bed you have admitted that you have not found the freedom you were looking for. You face, in saner moments, the sad truth: you have been irrevocably changed by quitting. If you are half the man we thought you were you are hating yourself for what you have done. The arguments you have adduced—you are being honest, you were living a lie while you were married, you finally got in touch with your real feelings and summoned the courage to defy convention and the expectations of all who love you—those arguments are beginning to ring hollow. You know that the "real feelings" of all of us nearly all the time are selfish, and what we conveniently call convention might be (in this case *is*) the clear command of God: "What God has joined together, man must not separate" (Matt. 19:6, NEB).

I earnestly hope that you have not fallen so far as not to be ashamed of yourself.

"In trying to extirpate Shame," wrote C. S. Lewis, "we have broken down one of the ramparts of the human spirit, madly exulting in the work as the Trojans exulted when they broke their walls and pulled the Horse into Troy. I do not know that there is anything to be done but to set about rebuilding as soon as we can. It is mad work to remove hypocrisy by removing the temptation to hypocrisy: the 'frankness' of people sunk below shame is a very cheap frankness" (*The Problem of Pain,* Macmillan, p. 45).

What you have done is detestable. Understandable, of course, but detestable. I know that from the Book. It says, "God hates divorce" (Mal. 2:16). If we do not also hate it we are not on God's side. I dare to hope that you still think of yourself as on His side, and are therefore, at least when you are not paying attention to the Enemy's suggestions, thoroughly ashamed. This is your hope of salvation. Until you accept God's estimate of the thing done, you will never seek His remedy.

Your present discontent is a mercy, affording opportunity to repent. Any inkling you have that all is not well is the still, small voice calling you back to repentance, reconciliation and restoration. Will you set about rebuilding as soon as you can?

The "Innocent" Party

A reader of the preceding letter said it was unduly harsh and did not seem to have any love in it. "I can't picture Jesus saying such a thing to anyone," he wrote. "It implies that Dick was bad and Sally was good."

Let's examine this for a minute. The harshness, I suppose, is inferred first because I said the news of the divorce was "like a kick in the stomach"—in other words, it hurt me personally. Any divorce ought to be bad news to a Christian because we know how God feels about it. This particular divorce was terrible news to me because I happen to love both Dick and Sally. If my letter to Dick seemed to my correspondent to have no love in it, perhaps that was because he imagines that love and judgment are mutually exclusive—if you love people, you will never say anything that will make them uncomfortable.

I wonder how attentively he has read the Gospels. Jesus often made people uneasy. Sometimes He made them furious. I wonder, too, how attentively my correspondent has read the letters of Paul, Peter and James. Those letters teach us clearly and strongly to call a thing what God calls it. If it's sin, call it sin. Deal with it as sin.

This goes for our own sins first, of course.

We are judged by the Word. It is the straight-edge that shows up our own crookedness. Let us confess our own sins, root them out, forsake them. Then, when we've done that (Jesus explained it vividly)—taken the "log" out of our own eye—we will be able to see well enough to take the "splinter" out of somebody else's. (Isn't it an act of kindness to take out a splinter for somebody?)

"Oh, come on, now—who do you think you are?" I hear someone saying, "What do you know about the situation between a husband and wife? You can't judge. Mind your own business!"

I said in my letter to Dick that there was much on both sides that I knew nothing about. I wrote to him solely about what I did know: he had made public vows, he had broken them. I hoped that there was still time to repent, to restore a relationship, to mend a shattered home and heal the appalling wounds of two little children.

But did I imply that Dick was bad and Sally was good? I did not. It is a very confused line of thought which says the guilt of one implies the innocence of the other. Let's assume that Sally was worse than Dick. He had promised to love and cherish her, for better or for worse. He broke that promise. That Dick sinned was clear enough and I said so. I did not say that Sally had not sinned. The person sinned against is not necessarily innocent. Far from it. Given the propensities of human nature, the very fact that one is sinned against dramatically enlarges the ordinary field of temptation to sin. I had no way of knowing how Sally might have sinned, but I supposed she did. I supposed that, being a woman, she is something like me. Full of pride, I would be dumbfounded, then hurt, devastated, furious and vindictive. I would feel extremely sorry for myself and would spend a good deal of time and emotional energy thinking of ways to retaliate, as well as to condemn Dick and justify myself. In other words, I could not possibly be called an innocent party.

Those are things I would be likely to have done when Dick told me he was leaving. The man who wrote to me suggested a list of things Sally might have done before and after his decision. "I challenge you," he wrote, "to write another letter to Sally about how she demanded things done her way, was often nasty and sarcastic, often used 'the good of the children' to get her way. How she used every trick to get her man hooked and then did not follow through. How she finally convinced Dick the children were better off without him than to be a constant source of quarrels. How she sort of liked being a heroine and making Dick look bad. How she had to build up her ego by being not only the nurturer of the children but the breadwinner as well. How she in her self-righteousness is going to bring up the children away from the bad influence of their dad."

Sally may be guilty of all these sins and more. Dick's list of offenses may be even longer. I do not know either side of the sad story. I am sure if I heard Sally's side my sympathies would be with her. If Dick told me his the very next day, my sympathies would promptly shift to him. I would conclude that both were right and both were wrong, there was a lot to be said on both sides, and we might as well throw up our hands and say, "Do your own thing. There's no way to work this out." Dick went to a psychologist who called himself a Christian (they tell me), who spent his time, not encouraging Dick to love Sally in obedience to God and thus to avoid divorce, but helping him "deal with his feelings" when the divorce happened.

I do not, I admit, know the story. But I know the One who knows it—all of it—and I know that *it is always possible to do what he tells us.*

The actress Katherine Hepburn had little patience for actors who surrendered to "the tortuous introspection of the Method," *Time* says. "You do what the script tells you," she said. "Deliver the goods without comment. Live it—do it—or shut up. After all, the writer is what's important."

That goes for us Christians. There *is* a Script. If there weren't, then we'd have to muddle through on our own, hoping by introspection and experiment to come up with something that might work. God hasn't left us to that method. He knew what we'd get into by sinning and has made provision for us. Let's live it—do it—or shut up and quit pretending to follow Christ. The issue we are discussing here is not whether Dick had good reason for unloading his family, but whether he had an option, according to the Script. "We never discussed a script," said Hepburn, "we just did it. Naturally and unconsciously we joined into what I call a musical necessity." Easier, I suppose, in theater than in the confusion and pain of a real marriage, but there is a "musical necessity" for all of us. Even when we cannot solve our problems, we can please God. Even when one person disobeys Him, the other can obey Him. My husband Lars and I know this is true. Poor students though we are ("fools and slow of heart to believe") we're daily trying to do our lessons in the school of faith and obedience, finding the truth of the old gospel song, "There's no other way to be happy in Jesus."

There is a common assumption today that

whatever we are and wherever we are is some-
how fixed and inevitable, while it is the
Ancient Word that must be bent. For example, a woman cheats a university by plagiariz-
ing and is refused a diploma. She decides she
has a right to the university's credentials even
though she happens to be a cheater; so she
sues. Another woman chooses abortion. It is
fixed and inevitable, in her mind, that what
might turn into a baby must be got rid of,
never mind the possibility that it's murder.
People protested the Abscam experiment because, after all, nobody can be expected to re-
sist *that* much money. To be loving, caring,
sharing and daring in the Christian commu-
nity too often means, for example, to tell Dick
he's O.K., he's got his own life to live, and to
tell Sally nobody can blame her for feeling sorry for herself.

"Blame"? The question here is, who assigns
blame? There is an Ancient Word, fixed, set-
tled, which shall stand forever. The present
situation is only grass which withers and flow-
ers which fade. We must quit bending the
Word to suit our situation. It is *we* who must
be bent to that Word, *our* necks that must bow
under the yoke. Love is no pleasing sentiment
but a fiery law: *thou shalt love.* In Dick and
Sally's predicament, I can only imagine how
deeply that fire will have to burn if they decide

to obey. I can imagine it, all right, for I know the sinfulness of my own heart and how much dross is there to be purified by the Refining Fire, how excruciating it is for me to submit to the Word that never permits the least indulgence of self-pity, self-vindication, self-aggrandizement, self-justification, or any other form of the self whatsoever.

A young woman called me the other day to describe what seemed an utterly insoluble marital problem. My heart was entirely with her. She lives with a man who seems to me and to many others "impossible." The things he asks her to do are unreasonable and absurd.

"He wants me to do so-and-so, but I'm not going to do it." I had little to say in reply, except that I would keep on praying for them.

"I guess you'd call that a stalemate, wouldn't you?"

I guessed I would. There was a pause. Then she said, "But, Elisabeth, you know, I have a strong feeling that it will remain a stalemate unless *I* do something. I think God is asking me to make the move, to submit to Jack. Do you think that would be right?"

"Yes."

"I don't think I can do it. I just can't do it. I keep hoping God will make it easy for me, but I guess He's not going to, huh?"

"Often in the Bible we find God bringing

people to a place of decision—often an 'impossible' decision (think of the Israelites in the Old Testament, the man with the withered hand in the New)—and at that point it's up to them. The refusal to obey when the choice is clear is the end of blessing," I said. "Obedience leads to some unimagined solution."

I knew how fearsome the choice was in her case. God knew it too. But God is the one who takes responsibility for the results when the choice is made in obedience. This is always the thing we can count on. Human relations present "impossible" difficulties. Sin seems to tie us into hopeless knots and we seek desperate solutions: divorce, abortion, lawsuits and every other kind of deliberate disobedience and wickedness. Of course, people understand. People sympathize. Some criticize, some judge as though they themselves would never be so tempted. This is wrong, and for me to say it is wrong is a *judgment*. It is not my opinion. It is the judgment of the Bible. The Bible tells us it is wrong to judge—not wrong to use our critical faculties, but wrong to set ourselves up as righteous and immune to the sin we are judging.

We have laid many traps for ourselves by forgetting how sinful we are and how badly we need the Script. We get into a mess and we declare ourselves bankrupt. Nobody can make any moral claims against us anymore. We are, spiritually speaking, out of business, closed. We're doing our thing, defying those who judge us, telling them it is always wrong to judge (which is in itself a judgment, but not one based on the Script).

My correspondent told me we should remember we've all broken vows, that Dick was doing the best he could and that I shouldn't make matters worse by making him feel bad, that I should love and care about him instead of criticizing so harshly. He said divorce was common in Bible times; it's better to separate than to live in hatred; and why don't we all just try to support the good and stop condemning the bad?

My correspondent was muddled. Trying to be humble and sensible and loving, I'm sure, but muddled nevertheless. Let's try to be clear. When sinful people live in the same world, and especially when they work in the same office or sleep in the same bed, they sin against each other. Troubles arise. Some of those troubles are very serious and not subject to easy solutions. God knows all about them, and knew about them long before they happened. He made provision for them. His Son bore all of them—all grief, all sorrow, all disease, all sin—for us. But why on earth (or in heaven) should He have done that? Why "should" He? He shouldn't, but He did. Because of love. The love that is stronger than sin, stronger than death.

And here is the profound lesson for us in the midst of our troubles. To rescue us out of them, Christ relinquished His rights. Are we His followers? Then let's take a hard look at what we have a right to expect from others. What does Sally rightfully expect from Dick? Love. "Husbands, love your wives." What does Dick rightfully expect from Sally? Submission and respect. "Wives, be subject to your husbands as to the Lord," and "the woman must see to it that she pays her husband all respect" (Eph. 5:25, 22, 33, NEB). What if the husband doesn't do what he's supposed to? What if the wife doesn't? Face up to it—in the world nobody gets what he is reasonably entitled to. There is the world's "solution" to this problem: fight. There is the Christian's: relinquish. God did not get what He had a right to expect—the love and obedience of the creature He had made. Instead He got rebellion and disobedience. Adam and Eve made a general mess of everything, and we carry on making new messes daily.

We have a Script. "Let your bearing towards one another arise out of your life in Christ Jesus. For the divine nature was his from the first; yet he did not think to snatch at equality with God, but made himself nothing, assuming the nature of a slave" (Phil. 2:5, 6, NEB). What Christ gave up was not His divine nature (people are always worried about losing their "personhood"), but the glory that nature entitled Him to. He was God by nature and He voluntarily became a slave, so that the Father could give back to Him in boundless measure the glory He had given up.

What a Script! What a lesson! Christianity insists always on *the rights of others.* A Christian lays down his own life to obtain them. If he asks, Have *I* no rights? the answer is "The servant is not greater than his Lord."

Selah, Sally. Ponder that, Dick. And God help me (Elisabeth) when the next test comes. It probably won't be more than five minutes from now.

Divorce and Other Questions

Every choice in life is made in some context. Not long ago I wrote a letter to a man named Dick who chose divorce. Then I wrote about Sally, the woman he turned loose, and about some of the choices she, the "victim," or the "innocent party," must make. Now I write to both of them—with trepidation, of course, aware that probably the last thing they want to hear about from me or anybody else is reconciliation. Hopelessness has perhaps set in by now, if not pure hatred, and they are convinced that everything has been tried and found wanting. The die is cast. The divorce is long since finished, and now they've got to get on with their separate lives.

The business of living a life for God is never finished, however, until we reach the gates of the City. ("Finished," did I say? But it is only then really begun!) I write to the man or woman in whose heart, even if that heart is broken or full of remorse and sin, still lies the longing to please God.

How can we do this? Well, let's not listen to any ungodly counsel. The man is called "blessed," which means *happy,* who walketh not in that kind of counsel (Psalm 1:1, AV). The trouble with the ungodly is that they have no reference-point but themselves, so they try everything that looks as though it might lead to a "solution." They leave out the one thing that really matters, the thing which, although not necessarily the direct route to solutions, is the only route to happiness. "Happy is the man who does not take the wicked for his guide, nor walk the road that sinners tread. . . . The law of the Lord is his delight" (Psalm 1:1, 2, NEB). That's what matters—the law of the Lord.

Not all who practice under the label "Christian" counselor are in the biblical sense godly.

There is sometimes uncertainty as to the authority and relevance of "the law of the Lord"—that is, of what the Bible says about human situations. "This is the 1980s," we are reminded. "There are no simple answers." I believe there are indeed some *simple* ones, but they are not *easy*. By that I mean that I can understand them—I cannot easily obey them. The road spoken of in that first psalm, the one sinners tread, is a wide one, smoothed by millions of feet. The road we must tread is narrow and rough, but we are not alone—the Holy Spirit has been "called alongside" to comfort, help, and teach us—and millions have walked the road of obedience before us.

If there is still a desire in the heart of either husband or wife for help, if there remains even the tiniest shred of forlorn hope that reconciliation is possible, might we ask first of all a question that precedes all other questions when godly counsel is sought? It is this: What is the context of our lives? There are two choices. We live our lives in the context of the world, which makes up its own rules as it goes along, or in the context of the Kingdom of God, in which the law is the Lord's.

What was the context of our conflict? Here we may run into difficulty. One or both partners may believe they did the will of God and that was what caused the conflict. Leave this one, then, and try the next: What did each of us do when the conflict arose? Was it dictated by concern for the Kingdom or God, or something else (personal happiness, perhaps)?

What is needed now to move into that heavenly Kingdom?

If both partners, humbly and honestly, answer that they want to live their lives in the context of the Kingdom, and are, humbly and honestly, prepared to pay the price exacted of those who live there, I believe with all my heart that there will be a "solution."

But suppose only one of them seeks God's will in the matter. It may be the one generally called the "innocent" party. He or she is being divorced by the other. Then again, the one claiming to seek God's will may be the one who filed the papers. He or she may have sought Christian counsel, prayed, tried to patch things up, and at last, in despair, turned to the law—that is, to divorce—as the only possible thing to do. *He* thinks of himself as the innocent one. There is yet another possibility— that the one who is seeking God's will is the one most acutely aware that he *is* at fault, that he is the *guilty* party.

What I have to say to this person, whichever he is, is not offered as a solution. God does not promise solutions to all our problems. The

gospel is not a guarantee of the healing of all
diseases, the dissolving of all debts, the mend-
ing of all marriages, and the fulfilling of all
desires *on this side of the Jordan.* The gospel, as
the good news of freedom from sin and self, is
in fact also a guarantee of what Jesus called
tribulation. You can't live as a Christian in a
sinful world without tribulation. Jesus came to
bring not peace but a sword. He described
Himself as a stone, rejected by the builders.
"Any man who falls on that stone will be
dashed to pieces; and if it falls on a man he
will be crushed by it" (Luke 20:18, NEB). Too
often we forget those stern words, or the
prophecy of old Simeon when Jesus was a
baby: "Many in Israel will stand or fall because
of him" (Luke 2:35, NEB).

What I have to say is infinitely more important than solutions. It is a matter of obedience.
In other words, if you are the one deeply longing for help, there are answers—answers
which will please God and enable you to do
His will. Will they "work"? you ask. The answer is yes—in terms of the Kingdom. But be
careful. The disciple cannot test the answers
in terms of earthly success or satisfaction or
solutions.

Obedience might in fact lead to reconciliation and thus to the miraculous repair of what
seemed a hopeless mess. But then it might not

lead to any such thing. Remember what Jesus promised to those who wanted to follow? "I have come to set fire to the earth. . . . Do you suppose that I came to establish peace on earth? No indeed, I have come to bring division" (Luke 12:49, 51, 52, NEB). "All will hate you for your allegiance to me. But not a hair of your head shall be lost" (Luke 21:17, 18, NEB).

What did He mean? He meant that sometimes there must be the choice between obedience and a solution—between His will and, for example, self-preservation. They are not always the same thing. As a matter of fact, in the Kingdom they often turn out to be quite opposite. "Whoever cares for his own safety is lost; but if a man will let himself be lost for my sake, that man is safe" (Luke 9:24, NEB). It's either/or. It's self-death and eternal life, or it's self-life and eternal death.

Divorce often seems the way not merely to happiness, but to simple survival and sanity. Not to divorce seems suicide. "This woman is ruining my entire career." "She's not a wife/he's not a husband." "This person is destroying my personhood." "Nobody can live with a woman like her."

It is clear that no direct action on your part will change another person. You can pray that

God will change him, and you can let God change you (you may be the one who needs it more!).

"No," you say, "it's hopeless. Divorce is the only way. Not to divorce would be suicide." What a dilemma! A thing God hates on one hand, suicide on the other.

I must walk very softly here. I have never been in this fix. I cannot say, "Our marriage was on the rocks and God worked a miracle for us." All I can say with confidence is that I have been in some other "fixes" in which obedience to God has appeared to be (humanly speaking) a terrible risk. At least once in my life it looked like "letting myself be lost." Suicide was not a word I used, because I was thinking in terms of Jesus' words quoted above, but it was certainly the word some people used regarding my decision.

Remember the martyr Stephen. It was witness that mattered, not self-preservation. Remember Shadrach, Meshach, and Abednego. It was witness that mattered, not self-preservation. I am not referring here to the popular use of the word *witness*—talking to somebody about his soul's salvation. I am speaking of a life laid down in obedience, whatever that obedience may entail. Such a life witnesses to love for God. One who loves Him does what He says, cost what it may. Not

a hair lost? No, not in terms of the Kingdom.
But yes, in the world's terms, more than
hair—the life itself—may be lost.

What, then, are the choices? I ask you gently
and in the name of Christ, what do you really
want? Is it Christ or happiness? Is it the will of
the Father, or is it freedom from pain? Is it the
Kingdom of Heaven or the kingdom of self?

If it is the Kingdom of Heaven you really
want, then you can do only what fits the terms
of that Kingdom. You will not be asking, "Will
this solve my problem?" or "What will I gain
by this?" or "What are my rights?" You will be
on your knees instead, saying, "Thy kingdom
come," which means "My kingdom go." You
will be saying, "Thy will be done," which
means "My will be undone."

"So you're saying it's absolutely wrong for
anybody to divorce anybody for any reason?"
No. "Well, then, what are you saying? What
am I supposed to do?"

So far I have been trying to encourage you
to think as a Christian. We are all deeply in-
fected by worldly patterns of thinking and
need constantly to bring our thoughts under
Christ's authority. Pray for guidance. Clear up
all that can be cleared up in your own heart
and conscience, remembering always to act in
the context of the Kingdom. The following
chart may help to clarify our choices.

Which Context?

The Kingdom of Heaven	*The Kingdom of Self*
Thy will be done (which means my will be undone)	My will be done (which means Thy will be undone)
Losing myself and saving what matters far more	Saving myself and losing what matters far more

My aims:
  another's happiness
   and fulfillment
  giving
  glorifying God
	my own happiness
	  and fulfillment
	getting
	satisfying myself

My object: eternal gain	temporal gain

My right:
  that of John 10:18
   to lay down my life
	to live life my way

My concern: obedience	solutions

The price:
  tribulation now,
   peace later,
  death to self,
   life forever
	tribulation later,
	  peace now,
	self-preservation,
	  death forever

Christians are members of the Body of Christ. As such they do not act alone or in isolation, but always with reference to other members. For a clear, biblical treatment of the many complexities of the questions which are beyond the scope of this article, see Jay E. Adams, *Marriage, Divorce, and Remarriage* (Presbyterian and Reformed Publishing Co., Phillipsburg, N.J.). Dr. Adams shows strongly the importance of the church's action in these matters. Discipline is the church's responsibility. Don't try to sort it all out alone. Go to the elders and deacons of a church where the Bible is believed to be authoritative and submit yourself to their ruling.

It is very likely that the first task assigned you will be repentance. Whether you are the one suing for divorce, or the one sued, you will have sinned *in some way, at some time,* against your spouse and against God. Confess every sin you can think of—every nasty thought, every sinful word or deed, everything left undone that should have been done, every attitude of rebellion and resentment and bitterness and hate. Confess them to God. Perhaps you will next have to confess to your spouse if he or she is still around and willing to listen. Remember the question asked early in this discussion—what is needed now to move into that heavenly Kingdom? This is it. Re-

worse ways to lose one!" I have no doubt about that. I am sure a much sorer wound results from rejection or unfaithfulness than from death. The healing of such a wound must be very deep, and, as with the healing of a physical wound, there may need to be both cutting and cleansing before there can be healing. The Word cuts. Taking heed to the Word cleanses. Then God (and only God) does the healing. He creates new life and new flesh. His forgiveness for us is as boundless and just as certain as it was for his disobedient people Israel, of whom He said, "I will bring them back to this place and let them dwell there undisturbed. They shall become my people and I will become their God" (Jer. 32:37, 38, NEB). It may be that the rest of that promise will be quite literally fulfilled as well: "I will give them one heart and one way of life so that they shall fear me at all times, for their own good and the good of their children after them" (vs. 39).

Does it seem impossible? Then perhaps you're still thinking in the context of this world. Try the other context, the one in which all things become new and even the dead are raised.

pentance. Turning around 180 degrees, and moving in the opposite direction. Taking a new route. Relinquishing the old.

After you have done that, you must forgive. You must forgive the other one even if he/she does not forgive you and cares not at all to be forgiven. I do not say you must give him/her a list of offenses which you are now going to cross off. Read the list only to God and cross them off in His presence. The items which your spouse knows about, which you have accused him of, you will probably need to forgive him for, specifically, to his face. No matter what he or she has done (and "sides" don't matter here—there is sin on both) you must forgive.

"Since unforgiveness roots itself down in hate, Satan has room for both feet in such a heart, with all the leeway action of such purchase. The word *unforgiving*! What a group of relatives it has, near and far! Jealousy, envy, bitterness, the cutting word, the polished shaft of sarcasm with the poisoned tip, the green eye, the acid saliva—what kinsfolk these!" (S. D. Gordon, *Quiet Talks on Prayer,* Revell, p. 79).

I have known what it is to lose a husband through death but not through divorce. When my first husband died, a newly divorced friend wrote, "Don't forget there are *much*